>TOURIST

GREATER THAN A TOURIST – HAVANA & VARADERO CUBA

50 Travel Tips from a Local

Facundo Iglesia

Facundo Iglesia

Greater Than a Tourist- Havana & Varadero Cuba Copyright © 2018 by CZYK Publishing LLC. All Rights Reserved.

All rights reserved. No part of this book may be reproduced in any form or by any electronic or mechanical means including information storage and retrieval systems, without permission in writing from the author. The only exception is by a reviewer, who may quote short excerpts in a review.

Cover designed by: Ivana Stamenkovic
Cover Image: https://pixabay.com/en/havana-cuba-capitol-building-1613263/

Greater Than a Tourist
Visit our website at www.GreaterThanaTourist.com

Lock Haven, PA
All rights reserved.
ISBN: 9781980974628

>TOURIST
50 TRAVEL TIPS FROM A LOCAL

Facundo Iglesia

>TOURIST

BOOK DESCRIPTION

Are you excited about planning your next trip?

Do you want to try something new?

Would you like some guidance from a local?

If you answered yes to any of these questions, then this Greater Than a Tourist book is for you.

Greater Than a Tourist- Havana & Varadero Cuba by Facundo Iglesia offers the inside scoop on Havana & Varadero. Most travel books tell you how to travel like a tourist. Although there is nothing wrong with that, as part of the Greater Than a Tourist series, this book will give you travel tips from someone who has lived at your next travel destination.

In these pages, you will discover advice that will help you throughout your stay. This book will not tell you exact addresses or store hours but instead will give you excitement and knowledge from a local that you may not find in other smaller print travel books.

Travel like a local. Slow down, stay in one place, and get to know the people and the culture. By the time you finish this book, you will be eager and prepared to travel to your next destination.

Facundo Iglesia

\>TOURIST

TABLE OF CONTENTS

BOOK DESCRIPTION
TABLE OF CONTENTS
DEDICATION
ABOUT THE AUTHOR
HOW TO USE THIS BOOK
FROM THE PUBLISHER
OUR STORY
WELCOME TO
\> TOURIST
INTRODUCTION
1. Let's Start with Money
2. Accesing The Interwebs
3. Go In Winter
4. Stay In Casas Particulares
5. Beware Of Jineteros
6. Here Be Some Transportation Tips
7. Eat On The Go Like A Cuban
8. Don't Drink (Water) Like A Cuban
9. Visit The Hotel Where The Mafia Used To Hang Out
10. Learn Some Revolutionary History
11. Admire Some Fine Art

12. Dance Like Nobody Is Watching
13. Listen To Some Jazz
14. Admire Some Art While Drinking, Dancing and Listening To Music
15. Love Seafood? Try these places
16. Discover The Afro-Cuban Culture
17. Smoke Some Cigars, Che Guevara Style
18. See The Best View Of The City
19. See The Second Best View Of The City
20. See The Best View Of The Galaxy
21. Take A Free Tour Through The Real Havana
22. Drink The Best Daiquiri On The Island
23. Drink The Best Mojito In Town
24. It's Coffee Time
25. Meet A Famous Caricaturist's Studio (And Probably Himself Too)
26. Learn How The 'Most Organised Country In The World' Really Works
27. Study In Cuba
28. See The Health System For Yourself
29. Buy The Cheapest Books In The World
30. Read A Book On The Beach
31. Admire A Fortification From The Age Of Pirates
32. Pray To Jesus Christ In Havana
33. Recharge Your Good Luck
34. Visit Ernest Hemingway's Old House

>TOURIST

35. Visit The Largest Cemetery In The Americas
36. Love Rum? There Is A Museum About It
37. Get Your Caricature Drawn While Drinking Beer
38. Eat Excellent Food at Excellent Prices In Paladares
39. Have A Cabaret Night
40. Visit A Groundbreaking Design Store
41. Walk Around The Malecón
42. Buy Souvenirs For Your Loved Ones
43. Spend A Day In The Most Beautiful Beaches In The World
44. Ride A Water Bike
45. Watch Extraordinary Florae And Fauna
46. Swim With Dolphins
47. Go Snorkeling In A Mesmerizing Cave
48. Meet Two Luxurious Mansions
49. Play Some Golf
50. Come Back

TOP REASONS TO BOOK THIS TRIP
50 THINGS TO KNOW ABOUT PACKING LIGHT FOR TRAVEL
Packing and Planning Tips
NOTES

>TOURIST

DEDICATION

This book is dedicated to
Joel and Matías, the best travel buddies ever
My family
Cubans all over the world.

Facundo Iglesia

ABOUT THE AUTHOR

Facundo Iglesia is a journalist who lives in Argentina. He has written for various newspapers there and worked in a few radio stations. He enjoys doing community work, reading and playing video games.

So no, he is technically not a Cuban local, but he travelled to the island a few times and is eager to go back, and thought that a book about Cuba should include tips from all the friends he made there and not just one person.

Facundo Iglesia

\>TOURIST

HOW TO USE THIS BOOK

The Greater Than a Tourist book series was written by someone who has lived in an area for over three months. The goal of this book is to help travelers either dream or experience different locations by providing opinions from a local. The author has made suggestions based on their own experiences. Please do your own research before traveling to the area in case the suggested places are unavailable.

Facundo Iglesia

FROM THE PUBLISHER

Traveling can be one of the most important parts of a person's life. The anticipation and memories that you have are some of the best. As a publisher of the Greater Than a Tourist book series, as well as the popular 50 Things to Know book series, we strive to help you learn about new places, spark your imagination, and inspire you. Wherever you are and whatever you do I wish you safe, fun, and inspiring travel.

Lisa Rusczyk Ed. D.
CZYK Publishing

Facundo Iglesia

OUR STORY

Traveling is a passion of the "Greater than a Tourist" series creator. Lisa studied abroad in college, and for their honeymoon Lisa and her husband toured Europe. During her travels to Malta, an older man tried to give her some advice based on his own experience living on the island since he was a young boy. She was not sure if she should talk to the stranger but was interested in his advice. When traveling to some places she was wary to talk to locals because she was afraid that they weren't being genuine. Through her travels, Lisa learned how much locals had to share with tourists. Lisa created the "Greater Than a Tourist" book series to help connect people with locals. A topic that locals are very passionate about sharing.

Facundo Iglesia

>TOURIST

WELCOME TO
> TOURIST

Facundo Iglesia

INTRODUCTION

"What do we leave behind when we cross each frontier? Each moment seems split in two: melancholy for what was left behind and the excitement of entering a new land."

— Ernesto Che Guevara

In 1939, Winston Churchill said that Russia, then a major part of the Soviet Union, was "a riddle, wrapped in a mystery, inside an enigma". Little did he know that, in 1959, a little island from the Caribbean would also be the land of a communistic revolution and that his words could also describe it very accurately.

Since the '90s, after the fall of the socialist block, Cuba became a fascinating destination for travelers from all around the world. Its beaches and its history attracted all kinds of people and awoke all kinds of interests. Cultural tourism interlinked with a more traditional leisure industry, but the curiosity of seeing a socialist country working (or not) is a major part of the "package".

Facundo Iglesia

So, here is a warning for all of you, that most likely come from a capitalist country and have a formed idea about Cuba before going there. Drop that. Don't go to the island with any kind of prejudice, good or bad. Allow yourself to be surprised by a country that's much more than its economic system, and even much more than its beaches.

If I could sum up all the 50 tips of this book in just one, it would be "speak to every person you see". We are talking of a really warm, well-instructed people, who are eager to share opinions and ask about the life in your country. Be honest with them, and be honest with yourself. Keep your eyes and ears open, fill yourself with Cuba and its culture, and try to resolve the enigma.

In this mysterious country, high quality, free healthcare and education live together with low incomes and difficulties to access to technology. Low insecurity rates live together with a State protection that can be a little overwhelming. One of the most educated populations in the world has to live together with overqualified workers, due mainly to the fact that the tourism industry is the most profitable activity of the country.

When you come back to your country, tell everyone about what you saw there, about the things

>TOURIST

you think are good and the things that you think are not: Cuba suffers from a certain degree of isolation, both geographical and political, both self-imposed and imposed from overseas and you, as a tourist, can help to break that. But your efforts will only be useful if you are totally honest about what you saw.

Facundo Iglesia

>TOURIST

1. LET'S START WITH MONEY

Money may not be the most important thing in the world, but it is still pretty relevant even in a communistic system like the Cuban one. And it can be a huge pain the back for tourists if you travel uninformed on that matter. So let's get to it:

First off, don't carry U.S. dollars to Cuba. There is a 10% anti-imperialist tax on the green bills when you change them to the local currency. For that reason, I recommend taking Euros, which will be accepted in all the bureaus de change. Since we are on that topic, I strongly advise you to change money only in the official exchange booths -which are called CADECAS-, since they offer the best rates. There is at least one CADECA in every town, and there is one in the José Martí Airport, so you can get right to it the moment you step out of the plane.

Cubans have two kinds of currency: CUC and CUP. CUP, or "peso nacional" is the one locals use to pay for transportation, food, medicine and other goods. CUC, or "peso convertible" is roughly equivalent to the American dollar and it is the one most tourists use. However, it is very useful to have a few CUPs in your pocket because some products are priced in the national currency and sometimes you will lose a few cents in the conversion. I would say that you should carry 70% of your money in CUCs and the remaining 30% in CUPs.

Also, you can use credit cards and some debit cards to pay for a few really specific things and to extract money from ATMs. You should check with your bank if yours is any good.

2. ACCESING THE INTERWEBS

So, now that we got you covered with the money problem, it's the turn for the second most important thing in the planet: The World Wide Web. You see, due mainly to the trade embargo imposed by the U.S., Cubans still do not count with free access to the Internet everywhere. However, it's not as bad as you may have read.

You can browse the Internet freely but only if you go to the designated areas (which are mainly parks, hotels, libraries, universities, etc.). Rule of thumb: when you see dozens of people using their mobile phones, you are in a Wi-Fi hotspot.

>TOURIST

Things are not that simple, though: you have to buy Internet minutes. You may do so in the ETECSA (the national communications bureau) offices. You get a card there (they are not cheap at all, so I highly recommend doing so in the official ETECSA bureaus, because you will get the best price there. Also, take your passport! They will ask you for it!), which you can scratch in order to get a username and a password. Then, you can connect to the "ETECSA" Wi-Fi network in the designated hotspot, and access it with the information on the card. And yes, the Internet in Cuba is free (as in "libre", definitely not as in "gratis"): You can access almost every site in the world.

3. GO IN WINTER

Yes, I know what you're thinking. "Cuba? In winter? What about the beaches? I want it to be hot!". Well, the coldest season in the year is a little different in a tropical island. For instance, it's not cold at all. We are talking about 20°C minimum temperatures, and even those are

Locals say that it wasn't always that way, and that sometimes, in winter, it was usual to see people wearing ushankas (Russian fur caps) and big, fuzzy jackets in the Island. However, nowadays the Island lives a "constant summer".

So, if you go during the summer things can get a little… sticky and very, very uncomfortable for us mortals. With temperatures that can up to 50°C, heat strokes are a very real possibility, for locals but especially for tourists that aren't accustomed to that kind of hotness. So, the best time to go? December to March. And that doesn't mean the sun won't strike you: So, follow my advice and take some sunscreen and bottled water wherever you go.

4. STAY IN CASAS PARTICULARES

What kind of trip are you taking? Do you want to be a regular tourist who only travels for the beautiful beaches or, instead, are you interested to see how life on the island really is like? In order to get the full Cuban experience, you should stay in Casas Particulares, or particular homes. They are a State-encouraged accommodation, that usually consists of a room in a house owned by a Cuban family. When it comes to Havana, I personally recommend staying in Vedado, which is one of the most beautiful neighborhoods in the city. In Vedado, the whole town will satisfy your needs.

Yes, maybe you won't have room service but you won't be staying in a shack either. Since they are State-controlled, you will get high quality rooms if you go to the official ones. Most of them also offer a fairly-priced complete breakfast. You may recognize them by seeing the symbol of the Casa Particular outside the house, which resembles a blue, rounded, upside down "H" letter.

But comfort and price aren't the only reasons for staying in a Casa Particular: They are an excellent opportunity to meet real Cubans and to talk about the life in the island, if you are interested in that kind of thing. People are generally very warm with the tourists and very open to answering questions. Also, expects some questions from their side! Prepare yourself for an excellent experience: I'm not exaggerating when I say the things I learned from those conversations shattered my worldview.

Facundo Iglesia

5. BEWARE OF JINETEROS

This is the only tip that has to do with security, and that's totally on purpose, since Cuba is one of the safest places on Earth. Very few actual robberies take place in the island, but there is other kind of "insecurity" and it doesn't have to do with gunpoint muggings. They are, simply put, scams. And a lot of them happen on the island.

The most common one is called "jineteada" or "horse riding". It consists of a local, usually a man, who will sweet-talk to you in order to convince you of giving them money or another valuable thing. They start by asking you where you are from and –this is very important- if this is the first time in Cuba or how long have you been in the island. It's crucial that you answer that you have been around at least a few weeks and that this is not your first time in the country, because that way you will not be seen as "naïve". Or, even better, don't answer at all.

The "jineteros" will also try to take you to bars, restaurants, night clubs and charge you a commission for it. They will sell you low quality tobacco, medicines and every kind of thing. They will try and sell you women, or pretend that they are in love with you. They will lie and tell you they have to buy diapers for their babies. The list of possible scams for tourists is so long, that it would fill up an entire book. So, when you suspect that a "jinetero" is trying to rip you off for being a "Yuma" (foreigner), just politely dismiss them. Don't let this ruin your trip: most Cubans are hard-working, nice and respectful to tourists.

6. HERE BE SOME TRANSPORTATION TIPS

Here you will be getting a bunch of tips for the price of one, since we are going to break down the types of transportation you can take within the city and beyond.

In first place, there are the *guaguas*, which are the city buses. Incredibly cheap and omnipresent, you may find them a little too small a too crowded, but they will get the job done. There are stops for them everywhere, and locals will be pleased to tell you which ones will take you to your destination. These is the means of transportation most locals use to move themselves on the city.

When it comes to taxis, things get a little trickier since there are various kinds of cabs. The State Taxis are generally new vehicles, yellow or white colored, and their license plates have a blue stripe, white background and black characters. On the other side, there are two kind of Private Taxis, which are generally well-maintained cars from the 50s: the collective ones (taxis colectivos), which take a pre-established route and pick up passengers similarly to a bus, and the personalized ones which will take you wherever you want. You can find the last ones in the Capitol area, or by asking in your hotel or casa particular. Bicitaxis (taxi-bikes) are also a choice, which is pretty self-explanatory: They are bicycles that can carry up to three passengers.

If you want to leave the city, Vía Azul buses will take you to every town in Cuba. In Havana, the station is located in the intersection of Ave.26 and Zoológico.

7. EAT ON THE GO LIKE A CUBAN

Tourism is one of the biggest contributors to the Cuban GDP, so it's only logical to expect lots of expensive restaurants in the capital (more on those

>TOURIST

later). However, if you want to grab some cheap food, you can do that as well.

There are lots of more-than-affordable places to get some chicken, pork, pizza, hamburgers, hot dogs or sea food. Maybe the decoration isn't as glamorous as that in establishments that were conceived for tourists, but the food quality is virtually the same or even better. Hidden in plain view across Havana, you should order in these places with some CUPs (see tip #1) in your pocket.

The 23rd Street in Vedado is particularly full with these kind of establishments. What food do I recommend the most? Well, Cubans aren't used to eating beef, because cows are scarce and reserved for children up to the age of 13. So, if you ask for a hamburger, it's probably pork. It takes a moment to get used to them if your country thinks cow when it thinks burgers, but they are delicious. I particularly like pepperoni burgers (*pan con hamburguesa y chorizo*). Also, as strange as it sounds for a Communistic country, pizzas are individual, but very yummy nevertheless! Bacon pizza (*pizza con bacon* or *pizza con tocineta*) is my favorite. Finally, we have to talk about hot dogs (*pan con perro*). Yes, Cuban hot dogs are spectacular, because the sausages are made with real meat. Now that I mention that, every food *is* real: very few additives are used and those ultra-processed foods we see in most other countries virtually don't exist here. Point for Cuba!

8. DON'T DRINK (WATER) LIKE A CUBAN

It's the turn for non-alcoholic beverages. I know, I know, booze is coming along. Be patient, please! But, as much as we love daiquiris and mojitos, we can all agree water is more important, right? Right?

Let's cut to the chase: don't drink tap water. At all. It has a high percentage of chlorine, and most human organisms aren't used to it, so it will make you very ill. I know a few foreigners that had to return to their countries after getting sick from the water, so take my word for it: Don't drink it! It's good for taking baths, doing dishes and washing your teeth though. So, where can you get drinking water? Most stores sell it bottled for a reasonable price. That one is safe to drink.

But there are some people that think that water is only for showers and toilets and prefer to consume sugarier beverages. So, in case you were wondering, yes, there are soft drinks in Cuba! And yes, you can get soda cans from the two main brands in the world.

>TOURIST

There is also a national one, Tu Kola, which is also pretty good.

However, the kings of cold, non-alcoholic beverages in Cuba are the juices (specially pineapple and orange ones, which are the tastiest!). In most countries, you couldn't get a natural juice anywhere but this is different in Cuba: Every juice you buy in a bar or a store is 100% natural, fresh and produced with agrotoxic-free fruit. So, for all the foodies out there, this island is an ideal destination!

9. VISIT THE HOTEL WHERE THE MAFIA USED TO HANG OUT

Now for the Godfather-y moment of your trip. In the '50s, Cuba was a paradise for the mob: bosses of international crime syndicates roamed around freely on an island filled with gambling and prostitution, and a government that was too happy to host them.

There is a place that is a symbol of those times: The Hotel Nacional, located in 0 and 21th streets, in Vedado. Inaugurated in 1930, this hotel is like a big monument to corruption and excess from a different era. But I can't lie: it's beautiful and you have to visit it!

It occupies the place where a 18th century defensive system of the city was set up. Nowadays, it's filled with pictures of those crime lords but also with images of politicians and artists who stayed there, there are tours that you can take to learn the story of the hotel which is linked to the Cuban one. Also, you can drink mojitos and smoke some habanos, but that's a given if you are in this island.

10. LEARN SOME REVOLUTIONARY HISTORY

Havana (and all of Cuba) is riddled with museums of all kind, art galleries, studios… Cuba is a really cultural country and that might constitute a surprise for tourists that go only in search of beaches. One of the most important historical museums is located in the colorful and picturesque Centro Histórico, specifically in 1 Refugio between Zulueta and Monserrate Streets. I am speaking of course about the Museo de la Revolución (The Museum of the Revolution) and the Memorial Granma.

>TOURIST

Formerly the residence of the presidents of the republic, the Museo de la Revolución is an eclectic and luxurious building that exhibits historical artifacts belonging to the rebellion that took down the Batista dictatorship in 1959. You can see letters written by the revolutionaries, newspapers from that time, firearms used by both sides of the struggle, and clothes worn by the protagonist of the fact that defined the road that the country took up to this day. The Museum also has a hyper realistic statue representing Che Guevara and Camilo Cienfuegos in the jungle. As with all museums, I highly recommend taking the tour with a guide, since most of the artifacts exposed may speak louder with the help of a local.

Located next to the Museo, the Memorial Granma preserves the original Granma yacht in which 82 young people navigated from Mexico to Cuba to start the Revolution. There also are land vehicles and airplanes used in the struggle. In both sites, there are living parts of history: You cannot go to Havana and miss them.

11. ADMIRE SOME FINE ART

Earlier I wrote that the Island is bursting with culture, but you don't have to take my word for it: If you want to check it for yourself you should definitely go to two of the most relevant art museums on the island. They are the two Museos Nacionales de Bellas Artes (National Museums of Fine Arts). One of them is dedicated to Cuban Art and the other one, to Universal Art.

The Cuban Art building (which is located in Trocadero between Zulueta and Monserrat streets) is an enormous, modern installation that feels as if you were travelling through all the history of Cuba: The exhibitions display pieces from the Colonial time up to contemporary art. Check out "La Silla" by Wilfredo Lam and "Gitana Tropical" by Cuban painter Víctor Manuel.

Near the Cuban Art building, you can find the one that has the Universal Art collection (San Rafael between Zulueta and Monserrat streets). If the previous museum gives you the feeling of travelling through Cuban history, here you will feel that you are visiting different stages from the development of

>TOURIST

Human kind. Roman and Egyptian art, some Goya, some Murillo... This Museum has it all, and the building is impressive. Tip within a tip: sightsee them with a guide! For people that are uninitiated in fine arts, some paintings and sculptures don't say much per se, but the guides are very well-instructed and can tell you what they really mean.

12. DANCE LIKE NOBODY IS WATCHING

Since we are talking about places that serve drinks named after Florida, you should definitely check out the Hotel Florida's bar, where you can have a lot of fun. While the admission fee is not that cheap, it includes some drinks to get you started. Why go there? The energy that flows in that place is really vibrating, and I think it has to do with the fact that tourists and locals mix. You can dance and listen to live music, but don't try to compete with Cubans: They are all experts at it! The hotel is located at the intersection between Obispo Street and Cuba Avenue.

Another place where you can show off your dance moves (and won't be ridiculed by locals, since it's an establishment that's mainly for tourists) is La Casa de la Música (The Music House). Actually, there are two Casas de la Música. One of them is located in Centro Habana (in Galiano St. between Concordia and Neptuno) and the other one in the Miramar neighborhood (3308 20th Ave.).

The Centro Habana version is more spacious and informal than the one in Miramar, but they both share a really frenetic atmosphere, where you can listen to live bands of music genres that range from salsa to hip hop. The two of them open at 10 pm and the price range varies, depending on who is playing that night. And in both of them, you can dance your shoes off until the sun is out.

13. LISTEN TO SOME JAZZ

Maybe dancing frenetically isn't your thing, and you prefer smoother music and a more intimate ambience. Search no more: in La Zorra y El Cuervo (The Fox and The Crow), you can listen to the best live Cuban jazz in the city.

Located in the basement of an apartment building, you can access La Zorra y El Cuervo from a British-style phone booth. And, while jazz is the main genre being played, you can also listen to the best salsa and

>TOURIST

timba performers while drinking an excellent mojito crafted by some of the most skilled hands in town.

House to many impressive international jam sessions, La Zorra y El Cuervo contributed to put Havana in most jazz tour circuits of the world. The place is so popular it's often crowded, so the best thing to do is to reserve a spot in advance. You will find this gorgeous music bar in the modern neighborhood of Vedado, in 23rd St. between N and O.

14. ADMIRE SOME ART WHILE DRINKING, DANCING AND LISTENING TO MUSIC

What if you could go to a night club that is also an art gallery that is also a restaurant that is also a theater that is also a live music display that is also…? In Havana, you can. Being in Fábrica de Arte Cubano (Cuban Art Factory) is, by far, the most fun I've ever had in a night club. It blows the mind of everybody who goes there.

DJ's live together with contemporary and experimental art. At the same time, you can watch performances and live music. It is a truly unique experience, the likes of which I had not seen anywhere else in the world. From the large building (a repurposed warehouse) where you can get easily lost, to the revolutionary (not in a Fidel Castro kind of way) art exhibits that happen at the same time, no visit to the Fábrica de Arte is the same. How so? Well, quite literally, because the labyrinthic installation changes in some weird, Harry Potter-style, so areas that may be open one day may be closed the next and viceversa.

Also, the food there. Good Lord. There are dishes from all over the world: Falafel, tapas, bruschettas… You name it! They are all professionally-made and not that expensive at all. You should go at 9 pm, if you don't want to wait in line for too long.

15. LOVE SEAFOOD? TRY THESE PLACES

When it comes to seafood (and trust me, it will come to seafood if you are in Cuba), there are two places that can't not be in your restaurant list. Yes, I tried to write only about one of them, but they are both excellent in their own way (and also, I love seafood! So, as I like to say, why not both?).

>TOURIST

Vistamar is one of Havana's best restaurants. One could say that its most striking feature is the beautiful view of the sea. Or maybe, the perfect ambience or the local music. But that hypothetical person would be wrong, as its strong suit is obviously the delicious seafood ceviche! Also, this venture an ideal paladar to go with your significant other, because of its romantic atmosphere. The address? 2206 1st Avenue, betwenn 22 and 24 streets.

On the other side, if you are not looking to spend a night with your loved one but still want to eat delicious seafood in an excellent, original ambience, you should go to Santy Pescador. It not only offers excellent fish, but all kinds of Japanese food. It's a little far from the city, and you probably will have to ask for directions (I won't believe you if you tell me that you can arrive without getting lost once). The place itself is marvelous, it's by the river and the fishermen boats and if you go to its rooftop you can take beautiful pictures. Recommended dishes? Ask for the lobster, the sushi or the ceviche. The address? 240A between 3C and Rio.

Facundo Iglesia

16. DISCOVER THE AFRO-CUBAN CULTURE

Are you planning on being in Havana on a Sunday? Then you can't miss El Callejón de Hamel (Hamel's Alley), an impressive community project linked to the Afrocuban culture, filled with murals by artist Salvador González, paintings, sculptures, installations and gastronomy.

This cultural landmark consists of an alley that was turned into a symbol of the city, because of its links to the afrocuban religion. González, the author of the murals, was the one who created this place in order to disseminate and preserve this popular culture, together with members of the afrocuban community. His paintings and sculptures, along with those by other artists, are on sale in the alley.

On Sunday's middays, the traditional rumba takes over the whole place, which is located between Aramburu and Hospital streets. And you know what rumba means: drumming, dancing and wholehearted spontaneity! Still looking for reasons to visit El Callejón? It was declared World Heritage by UNESCO in 2016. And you can't contradict UNESCO.

>TOURIST

17. SMOKE SOME CIGARS, CHE GUEVARA STYLE

Well, this is Cuba we are talking about! You are expected to receive some tips about tobacco. So, let's get to it. There's one thing that you don't have to do, and that's buying cigars from people on the streets. I've already mentioned that the Cuban economy depends greatly on tourism, and there are some people that want to take advantage of that. These self-proclaimed expert sellers will tell you things like "Today is the last day of the Big Tobacco Festival" (There isn't one) or "This was made by a Tobacco Cooperative" (There isn't one) and try to sell you cigars for more than they really cost. Just don't listen to them, and you will be fine.

So, where should you buy cigars? You have a number of options, but if you want to play safe, you can go to La Casa del Habano (The House of the Cuban Cigar), which is located in the Habana Libre Hotel's lobby (that's in L Street between 23 and 25 streets). You can buy 27 brands of Cuban cigars, and you have a walk-in humidor and personal lockers. Another choice is going directly to the source:

Another Casa del Habano is in the Partagás cigar factory. Although the real factory has been relocated, cigar lovers consider this a major destination because, besides the possibility of buying and smoking cigars while drinking a very good mojito, you can meet a master cigar roller here, whose real name is Hamlet. And no, I am not joking. This place is located in 520 Industria Street, between Dragones and Barcelona (behind the Capitol).

And if you really, really love cigars and you want to learn some things about them, you can go to the museum. The Museo del Tabaco y Casa del Habano, which is in 120 Mercaderes between Obispo and Obrapía streets, shows the history of the development of the tobacco industry on the island. And of course, you can find habanos in this museum's gift shop.

18. SEE THE BEST VIEW OF THE CITY

This is not your traditional panoramic view of the city: Here, you can see a big part of Havana, steampunk style: It feels like something straight out of a dystopian science fiction movie, but made with 14th century technology. I'm talking about the

\>TOURIST

Cámara Oscura (Dark Chamber), located in the Gómez Vila building, in Teniente Rey and Mercaderes streets.

Based on an optical effect, you can see in detail and in real time some of the most important buildings of Habana Vieja, on 360° images located in a concave screen in a completely black room. And all of this, through a periscope that once belonged to the Spanish Armada. The view is truly breathtaking but pictures are not allowed! Why? Well, let's say that sometimes, if you are lucky or unlucky, depending on your preferences, you may see some people in their balconies in rather embarrassing situations, and they would prefer you not to have a souvenir of that moment.

The Cámara Oscura is the first one of its kind in the Americas, and the twin of the Torre de Avira in Cadiz. While the view inside the Chamber is breathtaking, it is not the only way of seeing the best parts from Havana from above. That very tower, the Gómez Vila building, is the highest around the square and you can go to its rooftop to admire the city. And yes, you can take photos up there!

Facundo Iglesia

19. SEE THE SECOND BEST VIEW OF THE CITY

You probably saw the pictures of this square. Che Guevara and Camilo Cienfuego's giant faces in scultoric reliefs have become somewhat of a symbol of Cuba. But, as impressive as they truly are, there is much more to this place. First of all, the political significance is unavoidable: Fidel Castro has addressed more than a million Cubans simultaneously there in key dates such as the International Workers' Day (and sometimes his speeches there went for hours and hours!).

Embedded between Independencia Avenue and 20 de Mayo Street, two of the main arteries of the city, you cannot miss the gigantic statue of José Martí that watches over the square. With a height of almost 150 m, that tower offers an impressive viewpoint of Havana in its entire splendor. The square and the tower are often full of tourists (and cops!), so you will need a little patience to get through. But I guarantee you, it's totally worth it.

>TOURIST

20. SEE THE BEST VIEW OF THE GALAXY

The whole galaxy fits in Plaza Vieja, one of the squares located in the historical center of Havana. Yes, there is a beautiful planetarium in the city! Donated by the Japanese government and located inside the Space Teather, it has an impressive projector of 6,500 stars, a representation of the Big Bang, and an enormous sphere that represents the sun.

But that is not all: In this mandatory visit, you will be able to make an imaginary, 45-minute cosmic tour across the stars and you will observe the main planets in the solar system. This faux space travel encompasses all the 13 billion years the universe is and it explains its origin according to science.

The planetarium also has a variety of telescopes, an astronomic library, a theater, interactive games and its staff is formed by astronomers and physicists. Last but not least, the Cosmonautics Room offers information on Cuba's landmarks in this area, especially about the Russian-Cuban space flight of 1980 which transformed Arnaldo Tamayo in the first Latin American person to travel in space. This exciting adventure can be lived in 309 Mercaderes between Teniente Rey and Muralla Streets.

21. TAKE A FREE TOUR THROUGH THE REAL HAVANA

So you are here to meet the real Cuba? You want a real Cuban to tell you like it is, with its pros and cons? Well, you are in luck. Among all of the tourist circuits, you can find one particular tour that will satisfy your needs for authenticity. Go to the beautiful Parque Central (Central Park), which is the epicenter of Habana Vieja. Where is it? It's surrounded by Zuelata, Neptuna, Prado and San Martín streets. When do you have to go? You have two options: 10 am and 4 pm.

Once you are in the park at those designated times, go near to the José Martí monument (do not sit on its stairs!) you should search for people in umbrellas, which typically have inscriptions similar to "Havana Free Tour" or "Havana Free Walking Tour". These are the two groups that offer the tour, and they are made up of Cuban tourism students and graduates.

>TOURIST

Typically, they give two different tours: One of them will take you to the Morros (see tip#31 for more information) and the other is a trip through Habana Vieja. They give the two of them in English and Spanish. I recommend taking them both, since they are both very instructive, but it really comes down to what are you more interested: History or the present? If you like history, you should take the first one, since it's focused in some of the landmarks of the 19th century. The Habana Vieja tour, on the other hand, takes you to sites like the bodegas where Cubans get basic goods through their libreta de abastecimiento (supply book) since that system was implemented in 1963. Again, don't be afraid to ask as many questions as you want! Those tour guides, as Cubans in general, have a varying range of opinions on the government. Also, while there is a "free" on the title of this tip, this is not necessarily true. You can pay them as much as you want, and if you don't have any money you can take the tour anyway.

Facundo Iglesia

22. DRINK THE BEST DAIQUIRI ON THE ISLAND

Quick question, where was daiquiri invented? Quick answer: Duh, in Cuba! Long answer: This world famous drink was invented in The Floridita bar in Havana, where you can go to nowadays. So, yes, you can drink a daiquiri in the cradle of the daiquiri!

The Floridita is located in Monserrate and Obispo streets, and was founded in 1817 with the name of La Piña de Plata (The Silver Pineapple). This place is probably the oldest restaurant bar still standing in the whole world, but its cultural significance doesn't stop there: Brace yourself because yes, you can drink a daiquiri while feeling like an intellectual.

American writer and Nobel laureate Ernest Hemingway (1899-1961), author of novels such as For Whom The Bell Tolls, used to be a regular in The Floridita and the daiquiri was his favorite drink. You can see a statue of the novelist in the bar, and if you have a copy of The Old Man and The Sea, you can read it in the same place where his author probably had some of his best ideas for it.

>TOURIST

23. DRINK THE BEST MOJITO IN TOWN

It is often said that a visit to Havana is not complete if you didn't go to the bar and restaurant La Bodeguita Del Medio. For those of us who went there, that is particularly true! This place is a piece of living history, where some of the most relevant figures of Cuba passed by and enjoyed the best mojito in the city.

The place is an old cellar that belonged to Spanish immigrant Ángel Martínez, its walls are adorned with messages that the visitors leave. There is one that is unambiguously the most famous one, a writing that was supposedly left by American writer Ernest Hemingway that reads: "My mojito at the Bodeguita, my daiquiri at the Floridita". Is it a fake? Nobody really knows, but the mojito there is pretty good nevertheless.

The bar is at the front and the restaurant at the back, and it's often at full capacity, so you will have to be really patient to get a seat, but it's totally worth it. You can find the Bodeguita in 207 Empedrado between Cuba and San Ignacio streets.

Facundo Iglesia

24. IT'S COFFEE TIME

So, last night you drank mojitos, daiquiris and beer. How are you feeling? A little under the weather, maybe? Need to recharge some energy? Look no further: go to El Escorial coffee shop.

Sitting in a place with a really nice ambience reminiscing that of Parisian or Roman cafeterias, you can enjoy the best coffee on the city. And, if that's your thing, you can combine the coffee with a cigar! Just ask for a café criollo (creole coffee), which comes with a complimentary habano. The way both tastes combine in your mouth is indescribable, and an experience you have to live by yourself.

El Escorial is located in the gorgeous Plaza Vieja, which is even more gorgeous at night because of the way the light from lampposts falls into the cobblestones and, somehow, the main fountain is also much more colorful! So, great coffee, a great view, a great ambience and also low prices! What's the catch? Well, as the coffee beans are grinded on the spot, you will have to be very, very patient. The exact address? 317 Mercaderes Street.

>TOURIST

25. MEET A FAMOUS CARICATURIST'S STUDIO (AND PROBABLY HIMSELF TOO)

Not a fan of the high culture? Looking for some high quality visual arts, but with a more popular flavor? Or are you a fan of Ares? No, we are not talking about the God of War, but about Arístides E. Hernández Guerrero, AKA Ares.

This artist started his professional life as a psychiatrist, but then discovered than he could a different way to make people think: he became a self-teaching caricaturist, painter, illustrator and sculptor. And he is really good at all those things: for his prolific work, he has won more than 130 international prices.

You may not know his name, but you probably saw at least one of his pieces: "Cuba Post Castro" (Post-Castro Cuba) is one of his most famous creations, an illustration than depicts a society of people resembling the historical leader of the revolution, one that travelled around the world after Fidel Castro's death and became a symbol of what the island would become. That's not it, though: he has written 21 books and illustrated 80 more. The contents of his work often are political and philosophical.

But you can go where the magic happens: his studio, which has been the house of many expositions and contains two other community projects, is in 4 San Ignacio Street, between Chacón and Tejadillo in the neighborhood of Habana Vieja. If you are lucky, you can meet the man himself or people that work with him. You can also buy printed reproductions of his work: they make great posters!

26. LEARN HOW THE 'MOST ORGANISED COUNTRY IN THE WORLD' REALLY WORKS

If you have walking the streets of Havana and you have paying attention, maybe you have seen a sticker on some house doors that reads "Presidente del CDR" (President of the CDR). So, are you a curious person? Do you want to know what those letters stand for?

CDR stands for Comité de Defensa de la Revolución (Committee for the Defense of the Revolution). The CDRs are a mass organization that

>TOURIST

is present in each block of each Cuban city since 1960 (keep in mind that the Revolution triumphed in 1959). Each one of the blocks has a CDR president that is eligible by the vote of those who live there. They also have a National Coordinator, and it even has Parliamentary representation. So, what are the functions of this grassroots movement, created originally to defend the Revolution from bandits and foreign attacks?

Basically, we can separate the present activities of the Committee in three sections: territorial activities (such as building maintenance, street cleaning and recycling), security (such as keeping a registry of everybody who lives or is staying on the corresponding block, being attentive to counterrevolutionary actions and drug trafficking and night patrolling) and relationships with institutions (insertion of young people in work and education). So, if you see the sticker, ask in the house where you are staying. If you are interested, maybe the president of your local CDR wants to talk about their work!

Facundo Iglesia

27. STUDY IN CUBA

So, have you fallen in love with the Island, its culture, its beaches, its gastronomy? With its people? Do you want an excuse to come back, maybe not entirely as a tourist, but to learn some things? You can totally do that!

In first place, you should go to Universidad de La Habana (Havana University, located in San Lázaro and L, in the Vedado neighborhood), a beautiful, large set of buildings that have a great historical significance in the history of Cuba: in its stairs, Fidel Castro gave some of his famous speeches against the Batista dictatorship.

Wander around its faculties, converse with its teachers and students... If you go at night, sometimes there are concerts for the Cuban youth in its stairs. Also, you can even buy some books in libraries nearby and eat some great, cheap food in a paladar, both located in J street, behind the University (you have to go through the campus to get there). And in the 556th of that same street, you will find the Department of International Relations, where you can learn what you have to do to study there.

>TOURIST
28. SEE THE HEALTH SYSTEM FOR YOURSELF

Are you a doctor, a medical student or someone who has an interest in medicine for no particular reason? Cuban medicine is one of the best ones in the world, if not the best one. Not just for its gratuity (the country has universal healthcare for its population), but also for its quality and variety. For instance, the production of new medications and biotechnology is a big contributor to the Cuban GDP. Also, and you can treat yourself with Western or traditional methods.

This is not to say that it's a perfect system. Scarcity of some medications is pretty common, since some of them are produced by the U.S., a country whose companies are not allowed to commerce with Cuba. But overall, the system is still pretty great. You don't have to take my word for it: You can go to pharmacies (they are literally everywhere) and speak with the chemists so they can explain how the cutting edge technology lives along with traditional, herbal medicine.

You can also go to a hospital and maybe, if planets align and there is a person there than can give you an improvised tour (if you stress enough that you have valid motives for such a thing). I highly recommend going to the Hospital Hermanos Almejeiras (Almejeiras Brothers Hospital), a state of the art medical facility that deals with high complexity diseases. The hospital treats Cuban and foreign patients and is systematically well evaluated in polls. The mesmerizing, 79.500 m2 building is located between San Lázaro and Berloscaín streets in Centro Habana.

29. BUY THE CHEAPEST BOOKS IN THE WORLD

You may find yourself walking through the Plaza de Armas, the founding site of the Villa de San Cristóbal, heart of the city of Havana, admiring the late 16th century architecture and wondering how many stories developed in that very place... Well, you can read about them now!

If you want to buy books, you should make a stop in the Feria de publicaciones y curiosidades (Fair of publications and novelties), which once was in the Plaza and now it's located some blocks away from it. Why buy your books there? For a variety of reasons. First, the price. Yes, books in Cuba are among the cheapest in the world, because the access to culture has been a priority for the Revolution, that lowered the price of publications to half once it took power. But, in this particular fair, you can get your books for even a lower price than in most bookstores in the city. Also, you can (and you should!) bargain. A lot.

On the other side, you can get things there that you won't be able to find anywhere else. Rare editions of rarer books, most of them of political and historical content. In this realm, you should read The Bolivian Diaries by Ernesto Che Guevara (Fun fact: Cuban universities give that book for free to new doctors!) There is also fiction, of course! You can probably get your hands on some novels by Leonardo Padura, the best contemporary Cuban author. "El hombre que amaba a los perros" (The Man That Loved Dogs) is his best work to this date, and you should buy it.

But don't take my word for any of this: talk to the sellers there, who know everything about literature and can recommend you books based on what you want to read.

Facundo Iglesia

30. READ A BOOK ON THE BEACH

So, you have a big bag full o' books. What? Are you planning to reading them in your hostel? Boring! Hello, you are in Cuba! There are beaches there! You should take your newly-bought books to the Playas del Este (East Beaches). Without going too far from Havana, you can go see the sea and watch the sunset while sitting on fine, white sand.

Take the T3 bus, in front of the Hotel Inglaterra (Ave. Prado 416) and get off in the Hotel Tropicoco stop. In 30 minutes approximately, you will be there. Located in the municipality of Habana del Este, in order from the road from Havana, you will see the beaches of Bacuranao, Tarará, Mégano, Mar Azul, Santa María del Mar, Boca Ciega and Guanabo. They cover almost 50 km of coastline, and if reading is boring to you, there are facilities that offer activities of all kind for tourists.

>TOURIST

31. ADMIRE A FORTIFICATION FROM THE AGE OF PIRATES

Actually, they are two fortifications: One of them is the Castillo de los Tres Reyes del Morro (Castle of the 3 kings of El Morro) and the other is the Fortaleza de San Carlos de la Cabaña. They were built around the 17th century in order to stop the British invasions. Hoy en Today, they are a Historical Park, and you can find the Museum of Antique Arms together with the Che Guevara Cultural Center.

However, the main attraction is the "Cañonazo de las Nueve" (9 o'clock cannon shot), recreated by military men dressed with 18th century uniforms. It's a reminisce of the times Havana was surrounded by walls that closed at 9 pm.

The most emblematic point of the castle is the Lighthouse, which provides light to incoming ships since 1844. Its 30 meter height makes it an ideal place to watch the sunset, since you will have a wonderful panoramic view of the Malecón.

You can go in taxi through the tunnel or crossing the bay by the "Lanchita de Casablanca" boat, located in the coastline avenue of San Pedro.

Facundo Iglesia

32. PRAY TO JESUS CHRIST IN HAVANA

Even if you are not the Catholic type, you can't go to Havana and not visit the giant Christ that has become one of the typical postcards of the city. If you take the "Lanchita de Casablanca", the same boat that takes you the Morro in the coastline avenue of San Pedro, you can go admire, from a really short distance, the famous statue.

With an impressive height that's around 20 m, the statue was built in Rome and brought to Cuba in 67 pieces by sea. It was inaugurated on December 24, 1958: that's slightly more than a week before the triumph of the Revolution. It was always a symbol of the dispute of the Revolutionary Government with the Catholic church and, when the relationship between the two institutions normalized, Pope John Paul II visited it.

History aside, it's a magnificent piece of art and if you stand in its 2-meter base, you can appreciate a breathtaking view of the city and the bay, one of the best ones in Havana. Surrounded by a beautiful green space, "Christ, the Redeemer" is a must see.

>TOURIST

33. RECHARGE YOUR GOOD LUCK

You may find yourself admiring the San Francisco de Asís Church, in Habana Vieja, specifically between Amargura and Teniente Rey streets. Its impressive belfry, that was once the highest point in the city, is something that deserves to be seen while you are in Havana, apart from the Museum of Sacred Art that is housed in the church.

But once you are outside the building, my friend, that is where the true magic happens. You may notice a large amount of people gathered around a statue. "El Caballero de París" (The Gentleman from Paris) is a representation of one of the most emblematic characters that roamed the city of Havana.

His real name was José María López Lledín, a real person that arrived in Cuba from Galicia, during the beginnings of the 20th century. He worked in a wide variety of jobs, and legend has it that in the '50s he lost his mind, after being imprisoned for a crime he did not commit. After being freed, the government allowed him to eat for free in all the city's restaurants. True or not, there is a popular belief that touching the index finger of the statue will bring you good luck. I personally can't guarantee that, but millions of tourists and Cubans can: just take a close look of that finger and see how small it is compared to the rest of the statue. It wore off from all the people touching it!

34. VISIT ERNEST HEMINGWAY'S OLD HOUSE

There is a man that popped up several times through this book, that has been crucial to the cultural history of Cuba and isn't even a Cuban. We're talking, of course, about Ernest Hemingway, one of the most notable writers in America a probably the world. As you know, Hemingway lived in Cuba from 1940 to 1960.

Today and since 1962, his former residence works as a museum and was the first institution created in the world dedicated exclusively to the conservation and dissemination of the life and work of this genius who produced masterpieces of literature that are an obligated read.

The house, known popularly as "Finca Vigía" is also a small ecological reserve, because of the stuffed animals that were Ernest's hunting trophies. Filled with books and pictures that were there when "Papa Hemingway", as the Cubans call him, lived there is a mandatory stop if you are a fan of this writer: I swear, there is no other way to feel this close to the writer than by breathing the same aura as he did in Calle Vigía and Steinhart.

35. VISIT THE LARGEST CEMETERY IN THE AMERICAS

Yes, it is kind of weird that a place that's so directly associated with death can be a touristic attraction, but the Necrópolis Cristóbal Colón (Christopher Columbus Necropolis) has transcended its original functions and become kind of an open-air museum.

Home of thousands of daily visitors, it has an extension of 57 hectares and more than 500 funerary monuments, including mausoleums, chapels, galleries and, of course, tombs. Divided into 16 blocks, it has well-defined areas that not only mark the social category of those buried there, but they also are a different art style each.

Facundo Iglesia

Among the most famous personalities that are resting there, you can find photographer Alberto Korda (1928-2001), who was known for taking the famost portrait of Ernesto "Che" Guevara, writer Alejo Carpentier (1904-1980), one of the fundamental writers of the Spanish language and pianist Rubén González (1919-2003), from Buena Vista Social Club.

Care for some spooky legends? In this cemetery, you can find the tomb of "La Milagrosa" (the Miraculous Woman), who supposedly died during childbirth in 1901 and was buried with the remains of her creature at her feet. Years later, when the sarcophagus was open, her corpse was holding the deceased baby with her hands. Since then, her tomb has become a place of worship for women who want to become mothers.

The cemetery is located in Zapata and 12th streets.

>TOURIST

36. LOVE RUM? THERE IS A MUSEUM ABOUT IT

There are two kinds of people in this world: Those who like rum, and those who love it. People who like just drink it in Cuba Libres, mojitos or by itself. People who love it also drink it, but want to know everything about this delicious beverage made from sugarcane.

So, if you belong to the second group, Havana has a place just for you: the Museo del Ron Havana Club, between Sol and Muralla streets, is located in the former house of Count of Mortera and offers an interesting tour on the development of this industry, from its origins to these days, without being shy about the links with the slavery. Some of the guides will do a (really funny) humorous routine, so as with all the other museums, I recommend not walking through it by yourself.

However, the star of the show is an impressive model of a sugar factory as well tools that are used in the industry. Also, besides of a shop where you can buy –unsurprisingly- some rum, there is a bar where you can taste typical cocktails of the island. My favorite is also one of the hardest to pronounce: Canchánchara.

37. GET YOUR CARICATURE DRAWN WHILE DRINKING BEER

Maybe you are in Plaza Vieja, admiring the fountain, chatting with the locals, watching the children play, ending a day after taking part in lots of fun activities. So, you may want to relax a little and drink a beer. Look no further: go to Cervecería Artesanal (Craft Beer House), in front of the Escorial Café.

The comfortable open-air ambience, sometimes accompanied by live Cuban music, is ideal for an afternoon drink. Albeit a little pricey, the craft beers are delicious (especially the dark blonde and the dark ones). Also, if you are totally crazy and not a fan of craft beers, you can drink the national industrial ones: Bucanero and Cristal, which are also pretty good. You can accompany any of them with some excellent chicken brochettes.

Also, although it's not a sure thing, caricaturists use to roam around the joint, drawing the unsuspecting patrons. If you're lucky, they will come directly to you and hand over the piece, and you should leave a customary tip for their work. A final warning: while accurate, their drawings may not be very… flattering. So, accept them only if you are boosting with self-confidence!

38. EAT EXCELLENT FOOD AT EXCELLENT PRICES IN PALADARES

A paladar (literally, "palate" in Spanish) is what Cubans call somewhat improvised restaurants, usually emplaced at the entryway of a family home, that offer cheap and quality food, and the possibility to meet some Cubans.

They typically consist of a few tables and chairs organized at the sidewalk or in a house's lobby. The prices are much lower than those of fancy restaurants, and the food is, as you may suspect, home-made in the most literal sense of the word. These kind of establishments are literally everywhere in every Cuban city, but I can recommend what I consider the greatest one in Havana.

Facundo Iglesia

El Vampirito (The Little Vampire) is the best paladar in Havana in terms of price-quality ratio. You will probably fall in love with the place. It's a little under the street level, so it's very well ventilated, and its decoration is eye candy and very original, and their staff is really nice and serviceable. And it has something that's hard to come across: total transparency in the food elaboration process, because you can watch everything that happens in the kitchen from your table. And the food? There is a wide variety of dishes: the Italian is particularly good, but the chicken, bacon and cream cheese sandwich is a must-try (which itself is a variation on the traditional Cuban sandwich). Also, there are some more conventional dishes, such as the mouthwatering smoked pork ribs, which come with a side of grilled vegetables and congri (rice with black beans). Do you want something to drink? Any juice or shake will do. The address? 6th street between 19 and 21, in Vedado.

>TOURIST

39. HAVE A CABARET NIGHT

You can't miss Cabaret Tropicana, a famous Cuban cabaret built in 1939, famous for its Arcos 41thde Cristal open air front. Even in the present day, it maintains all the most relevant characteristics of a cabaret show, so you will feel in a time capsule. To enjoy the spectacle, have in mind all the time that you will be watching the stage where artists such as Nat King Cole, Rita Montaner and Josephine Baker performed. Regarded as one of the best cabarets in the continent, the "Paradise Under The Stars" is in 72nd street between 41st and 45th streets.

40. VISIT A GROUNDBREAKING DESIGN STORE

Cuba is home to a great deal of different cultural expressions, as its youth is a very active sector of the society, expressing discomfort or approval towards the government, but always in an original way. And more often than not, young Cubans engage in cultural activities that aren't directly related to the Revolution, but are a vital part of the artistic life of the island. Sometimes, those activities also derive in beautiful objects that can make up for excellent gifts (or self-gifts).

    Clandestina is a design store, that is primarily known for its clothes, that usually contain a poignant Cuban phrase either in English or Spanish. For example, one of the most famous products is a t-shirt that reads "Lo malo de ser gay es contárselo a los padres" ("The bad thing about being gay is telling your parents about it").

    However, garments aren't the only thing you can find here. Stickers, posters, paintings, city maps, bags… all kind of design objects that have a lot of creativity embedded in them. The store is really small, but if you pass by it, it will surely call your attention, because its exterior really stands out: a metal t-shirt with the phrase "99% Diseño Cubano" (99% Cuban Design) is hanging above the door. Also, the store is the studio were they think and produce the things they sell, so you can talk with the designers themselves. Clandestina is located in 403 Villegas St., between Teniente Rey and Muralla.

>TOURIST

41. WALK AROUND THE MALECÓN

The Malecón is the concrete stripe that tries to contain the fury of the sea waves that constantly crash against the city. The Malecón sorrounds almost 8 km of the north coast of Havana. The Malecón started its construction in 1902. The Malecón is, without a doubt, very, very, ugly. "Havana's Sofa", as Cubans call it, is as aesthetical as a portable toilet in a rainforest. However, why can't I stop walking around it, knowing there was an almost certain chance of getting totally wet? And what is the best way of doing that (walking around it, not getting wet)?

Well, I would say: let it flow. Pick a nice, sunny day, grab a beer (I would say a strong Bucanero) and sit on the "sofa". Just chill and let the Malecón's magic come to you. People will surely ask what you are doing there, and you can chat with the locals that hang out there.

No, I won't change my mind: it is really ugly, but filled with life. Fishermen sink their fishing rods in the sea, get drunk and contemplate their existence. Musicians play their guitars, butchering a song by Silvio Rodríguez. Rappers, well, rap. It's really something else, and if you can get pass the ugliness of it, you will live an experience unlike any other.

42. BUY SOUVENIRS FOR YOUR LOVED ONES

In all likelihood, you have seen potential souvenirs while walking through the city. Moreover, in some of the places listed in this book, you can buy things such as posters, postcards, cigars, rum… Those can be good gifts, but maybe you want to find all of that and more in just one place.

Look no further: the best place for buying every kind of gifts is Almacenes de San José (San José Stores). This enormous department store used to be a portside warehouse from its construction in 1885 to 2009, when it was reopened after a 3-year restoration process. Now it's filled with dozens of stands that sell handicrafts, shirts, art pieces, fridge magnets...

Everything here is at the best price in town (and more so if you know how to bargain!) and the employees are very nice. Take some time to walk around all of the building, and to chat with some of the most talented artists in Havana. And if walking and talking makes you thirsty, you can also buy a coconut shake there!

>TOURIST

43. SPEND A DAY IN THE MOST BEAUTIFUL BEACHES IN THE WORLD

You may have gone to the Playas del Este and that's fine, they are beautiful beaches where you can have a really good time. But something is missing, right? They are not quite like the ones you saw in posters, postcards or surfing the Internet. The sand is not as white; the sea is not as blue. What's wrong? Was it all a lie?

No: the hand drawn-like beaches are all over Cuba, but the best ones are in Varadero. How can you get there? Well, you can look for tip #6 on transportation. Go to the Via Azul terminal and for a ticket to Varadero. You should plan staying at least two days in that city, and, as in Havana, you can stay in casas particulares but the norm is accommodating in all-inclusive hotels.

Once you arrive to Varadero, the beaches are to walking distance from the city center. The first time you see those drop-dead gorgeous landscapes, you may think you are dreaming, but that's not the case: you are in Varadero.

44. RIDE A WATER BIKE

Varadero is not just a ridiculously beautiful beach: you can also find the Parque Retiro Josone, a magnificent garden designed and built in 1942. It currently is one of the most visited places in the town, with its restaurants, bars and a lake with geese where you can take a ride on water bikes. It also has a tunnel below the 1st Avenue that leads directly into the beach.

The park is located in 1st Avenue between 54th and 59th streets.

45. WATCH EXTRAORDINARY FLORAE AND FAUNA

Since you are in Varadero, you should take an excursion to the Varahicacos Ecological Reserve. The reserve, which covers around 450 hectares, is characterized by a number of caves such as the Cueva de los Musulmanes and the Cueva de Ambrosio, which has aboriginal pictograms drawn on it. The Salina La Calavera (Skull Saltworks) is also there, and is considered to be the first one exploited by the Spaniards in America.

The tour through the caves is approximately 2 hours long, and the rocky formations are mesmerizing, but you can also watch autochthone birds, iguanas and non-venomous snakes. Don't be afraid! The animals aren't dangerous. There is also one of the caves that has bats in it, and you most certainly feel like Bruce Wayne or Indiana Jones when they come to you!

You can go there in a tour bus that you take in the terminal.

46. SWIM WITH DOLPHINS

The Varadero Dolphinarium is located in a coral lagoon, 400 m from the Chapelín Marina. It is an unmissable attraction that allows you to swim with these highly intelligent and sweet sea mammals. They jump, they kiss you, the only thing that they don't do is speaking! There are only two shows in the day, so if you want to enjoy this interesting spectacle you should reserve it in advance. I recommend going to the Infotur (between 1ST Avenue and 13th street) for more information on transportation and schedule.

47. GO SNORKELING IN A MESMERIZING CAVE

Want to feel like if you were in the center of the earth? Stalactites, Stalagmites, crystalline water in which you can submerge and feel renovated… The Saturno Cave will blow your mind. You should take a water-proof case for your camera, because the pictures you can take there don't have an equal anywhere else in the world. To book this trip, you should go to Infotur (see tip #48).

48. MEET TWO LUXURIOUS MANSIONS

They are many sophisticated, big houses in Varadero but two stand out: The Varadero Museum (57th Street and Playa Avenue) and the Xanadu Mansion (Carretera de las Américas km. 8 ½).

The Varadero Museum is a bungalow-style mansion that was once the summer house of engineer Leopoldo Albreu. It exhibits archeological remains, pieces related to the campaign which the Revolution lead in all of the country to fight illiteracy, together with collections of natural science.

The Xanadú Mansion is located on the rocks of San Bernardino, and it was built by excentric billionaire Alfred Dupont, who based its design in a poem describing Kublai Khan's palace. Built between 1920 and 190, you can go to Las Américas Restaurant, which is really price, but has the best cuisine of Varadero.

49. PLAY SOME GOLF

In Carretera de las Américas km 8 ½, there is a 18-hole 72 par golf course for the fans of this sport. With an area of 180 hectares and located meters from the coastline, it's filled with palms, ponds and bridges.

If you book it in advance, you can play there, if there is not a tournament going on, which is a pretty common thing: the classic Torneo por el día de la Hispanidad is host there regularly. Again, for more information, go to the Infotur offices (see tip #48).

Facundo Iglesia

50. COME BACK

Did you have a good time? Did you bond with the owners of the casas particulares you stayed in? Did you feel like you didn't have enough time to do everything you wanted to do?

Go back to Cuba and visit the people you met there. They will remember you, even if they meet many tourists, each one is special. This is a trip that you won't easily forget, and the locals that you met in the island won't either.

>TOURIST

TOP REASONS TO BOOK THIS TRIP

Beaches: Cuban beaches have no competence anywhere in the world.

Culture: There is virtually a museum or an art gallery in every block.

People: Warm and well educated, the Cuban people will feel like your own family.

Facundo Iglesia

>TOURIST

Bonus Book

50 THINGS TO KNOW ABOUT PACKING LIGHT FOR TRAVEL

Pack the Right Way Every Time

Author: Manidipa Bhattacharyya

Facundo Iglesia

First Published in 2015 by Dr. Lisa Rusczyk. Copyright 2015. All Rights Reserved. No part of this publication may be reproduced, including scanning and photocopying, or distributed in any form or by any means, electronic or mechanical, or stored in a database or retrieval system without prior written permission from the publisher.

Disclaimer: The publisher has put forth an effort in preparing and arranging this book. The information provided herein by the author is provided "as is". Use this information at your own risk. The publisher is not a licensed doctor. Consult your doctor before engaging in any medical activities. The publisher and author disclaim any liabilities for any loss of profit or commercial or personal damages resulting from the information contained in this book.

Edited by Melanie Howthorne

Introduction

*He who would travel happily
must travel light.*

-Antoine de Saint-Exupéry

Travel takes you to different places from seas and mountains to deserts and much more. In your travels you get to interact with different people and their cultures. You will, however, enjoy the sights and interact positively with these new people even more, if you are travelling light.

When you travel light your mind can be free from worry about your belongings. You do not have to spend precious vacation time waiting for your luggage to arrive after a long flight. There is be no chance of your bags going missing and the best part is that you need not pay a fee for checked baggage.

People who have mastered this art of packing light will root for you to take only one carry-on, wherever you go. However, many people can find it really hard to pack light. More so if you are travelling with children. Differentiating between "must have" and "just in case" items is the starting point. There will be ample shopping avenues at your destination which are just waiting to be explored.

Facundo Iglesia

This book will show you 'packing' in a new 'light' – pun intended – and help you to embrace light packing practices for all of your future travels.

Off to packing!

Dedication

I dedicate this book to all the travel buffs that I know, who have given me great insights into the contents of their backpacks.

About The Author

Manidipa Bhattacharyya is a creative writer and editor, with an education in English literature and Linguistics. After working in the IT industry for seven long years she decided to call it quits and follow her heart instead. Manidipa has been ghost writing, editing, proof reading and doing secondary research services for many story tellers and article writers for about three years. She stays in Kolkata, India with her husband and a busy two year old. In her own time Manidipa enjoys travelling, photography and writing flash fiction.

Manidipa believes in travelling light and never carries anything that she couldn't haul herself on a trip. However, travelling with her child changed the scenario. She seemed to carry the entire world with her for the baby on the first two trips. But good sense prevailed and she is again working her way to becoming a light traveler, this time with a kid.

Facundo Iglesia

The Right Travel Gear

1. Choose Your Travel Gear Carefully

While selecting your travel gear, pick items that are light weight, durable and most importantly, easy to carry. There are cases with wheels so you can drag them along – these are usually on the heavy side because of the trolley. Alternatively a backpack that you can carry comfortably on your back, or even a duffel bag that you can carry easily by hand or sling across your body are also great options. Whatever you choose, one thing to keep in mind is that the luggage itself should not weigh a ton, this will give you the flexibility to bring along one extra pair of shoes if you so desire.

2. Carry The Minimum Number Of Bags

Selecting light weight luggage is not everything. You need to restrict the number of bags you carry as well. One carry-on size bag is ideal for light travel. Most carriers allow one cabin baggage plus one purse, handbag or camera bag as long as it slides under the seat in front. So technically, you can carry two items of luggage without checking them in.

3. Pack One Extra Bag

Always pack one extra empty bag along with your essential items. This could be a very light weight duffel bag or even a sturdy tote bag which takes up minimal space. In the event that you end up buying a lot of souvenirs, you already have a handy bag to stuff all that into and do not have to spend time hunting for an appropriate bag.

> *I'm very strict with my packing and have everything in its right place. I never change a rule. I hardly use anything in the hotel room. I wheel my own wardrobe in and that's it.*
>
> Charlie Watts

Clothes & Accessories

4. Plan Ahead

Figure out in advance what you plan to do on your trip. That will help you to pick that one dress you need for the occasion. If you are going to attend a wedding then you have to carry formal wear. If not, you can ditch the gown for something lighter that will be comfortable during long walks or on the beach.

5. Wear That Jacket

Remember that wearing items will not add extra luggage for your air travel. So wear that bulky jacket that you plan to carry for your trip. This saves space and can also help keep you warm during the chilly flight.

6. Mix and Match

Carry clothes that can be interchangeably used to reinvent your look. Find one top that goes well with a couple of pairs of pants or skirts. Use tops, shirts and jackets wisely along with other accessories like a scarf or a stole to create a new look.

7. Choose Your Fabric Wisely

Stuffing clothes in cramped bags definitely takes its toll which results in wrinkles. It is best to carry wrinkle free, synthetic clothes or merino tops. This will eliminate the need for that small iron you usually bring along.

8. Ditch Clothes Pack Underwear

Pack more underwear and socks. These are the things that will give you a fresh feel even if you do not get a chance to wear fresh clothes. Moreover these are easy to wash and can be dried inside the hotel room itself.

9. Choose Dark Over Light

While picking your clothes choose dark coloured ones. They are easy to colour coordinate and can last longer before needing a wash. Accidental food spills and dirt from the road are less visible on darker clothes.

10. Wear Your Jeans

Take only one pair of Jeans with you, which you should wear on the flight. Remember to pick a pair that can be worn for sightseeing trips and is equally eloquent for dinner. You can add variety by adding light weight cargoes and chinos.

11. Carry Smart Accessories

The right accessory can give you a fresh look even with the same old dress. An intelligent neck-piece, a couple of bright scarves, stoles or a sarong can be used in a number of ways to add variety to your clothing. These light weight beauties can double up as a nursing cover, a light blanket, beach wear, a modesty cover for visiting places of worship, and also makes for an enthralling game of peek-a-boo.

12. Learn To Fold Your Garments

Seasoned travellers all swear by rolling their clothes for compact and wrinkle free packing. Bundle packing, where you roll the clothes around a central object as if tying it up, is also a popular method of compact and wrinkle free packing. Stacking folded clothes one on top of another is a big no-no as it makes creases extreme and they are difficult to get rid of without ironing.

13. Wash Your Dirty Laundry

One of the ways to avoid carrying loads of clothes is to wash the clothes you carry. At some places you might get to use the laundry services or a Laundromat but if you are in a pinch, best solution is to wash them yourself. If that is the plan then carrying quick drying clothes is highly recommended, which most often also happen to be the wrinkle free variety.

14. Leave Those Towels Behind

Regular towels take up a lot of space, are heavy and take ages to dry out. If you are staying at hotels they will provide you with towels anyway. If you are travelling to a remote place, where the availability of towels look doubtful, carry a light weight travel towel of viscose material to do the job.

15. Use A Compression Bag

Compression bags are getting lots of recommendation now days from regular travellers. These are useful for saving space in your luggage when you have to pack bulky dresses. While packing for the return trip, get help from the hotel staff to arrange a vacuum cleaner.

Footwear

16. Put On Your Hiking Boots

If you have plans to go hiking or trekking during your trip, you will need those bulky hiking boots. The best way to carry them is to wear them on flight to save space and luggage weight. You can remove the boots once inside and be comfortable in your socks.

17. Picking The Right Shoes

Shoes are often the bulkiest items, along with being the dainty if you are a female. They need care and take up a lot of space in your luggage. It is advisable therefore to pick shoes very carefully. If you plan to do a lot of walking and site seeing, then wearing a pair of comfortable walking shoes are a must. For more formal occasions you can carry durable, light weight flats which will not take up much space.

18. Stuff Shoes

If you happen to pack a pair of shoes, ensure you utilize their hollow insides. Tuck small items like rolled up socks or belts to save space. They will also be easy to find.

Toiletries
19. Stashing Toiletries

Carry only absolute necessities. Airline rules dictate that for one carry-on bag, liquids and gels must be in 3.4 ounce (100ml) bottles or less, and must be packed in a one quart zip-lock bag. If you are planning to stay in a hotel, the basic things will be provided for you. It's best is to buy the rest from the local market at your destination.

20. Take Along Tampons

Tampons are a hard to find item in a lot of countries. Figure out how many you need and pack accordingly. For longer stays you can buy them online and have them delivered to where you are staying.

21. Get Pampered Before You Travel

Some avid travellers suggest getting a pedicure and manicure just the day before travelling. This not only gives you a well kept look, you also save the trouble of packing nail polish. Remember, every little bit of weight reduced adds up.

Electronics
22. Lugging Along Electronics

Electronics have a large role to play in our lives today. Most of us cannot imagine our lives away from our phones, laptops or tablets. However while travelling, one must consider the amount of weight these electronics add to our luggage. Thankfully smart phones come along with all the essentials tools like a camera, email access, picture editing tools and more. They are smart to the point of eliminating the need to carry multiple gadgets. Choose a smart phone that suits all your requirements and travel with the world in your palms or pocket.

23. Reduce the Number of Chargers

If you do travel with multiple electronic devices, you will have to bear the additional burden of carrying all their chargers too. Check if a single charger can be used for multiple devices. You might also consider investing in a pocket charger. These small devices support multiple devices while keeping you charged on the go.

24. Travel Friendly Apps

Along with smart phones come numerous apps, which are immensely helpful in our travels. You name it and you have an app for it at hand – take pictures, sharing with friends and family, torch to light dark roads, maps, checking flight/train times, find hotels and many other things. Use these smart alternatives to traditional items like books to eliminate weight and save space.

I get ideas about what's essential when packing my suitcase.

-Diane von Furstenberg

Travelling With Kids

25. Bring Along the Stroller

Kids might enjoy walking for a while but they soon tire out and a stroller is the just the right thing for them to rest in while you continue your tour. Strollers also double duty as a luggage carrier and shopping bag holder. Remember to pick a light weight, easy to handle brand of stroller. Better yet, find out in advance if you can rent a stroller at your destination.

26. Bring Only Enough Diapers for Your Trip

Diapers take up a lot of space and add to the weight of your luggage. Therefore it is advisable to carry just enough diapers to last through the trip and a few for afterwards, till you buy fresh stock at your destination. Unless of course you are travelling to a really remote area, in which case you have no choice but to carry the load. Otherwise diapers are something you will find pretty easily.

27. Take Only A Couple Of Toys

Children are easily attracted by new things in their environment. While travelling they will find numerous 'new' objects to scrutinize and play with. Packing just one favorite toy is enough, or if there is no favorite toy leave out all of them in favor of stories or imaginary games.

28. Carry Kid Friendly Snacks

Create a small snack counter in your bag to store away quick bites for those sudden hunger pangs. Depending on the child's age this could include chocolates, raisins, dry fruits, granola bars or biscuits. Also keep a bottle of water handy for your little one. These things do not add much weight and can be adjusted in a handbag or knapsack.

29. Games to Carry

Create some travel specific, imaginary games if you have slightly grown up children, like spot the attractions. Keep a coloring book and colors handy for in-flight or hotel time. Apps on your smart phone can keep the children engaged with cartoons and story books. Older children are often entertained by games available on phones or tablets. This cuts the weight of luggage down while keeping the kids entertained.

30. Let the Kids Carry Their Load

A good thing is to start early sharing of responsibilities. Let your child pick a bag of his or her choice and pack it themselves. Keep tabs on what they are stuffing in their bags by asking if they will be using that item on the trip. It could start out being just an entertainment bag initially but with growing years they will learn to sort the useful from the superfluous. Children as little as four can maneuver a small trolley suitcase like a pro- their experience in pull along toys credit. If you are worried that you may be pulling it for them, you may want to start with a backpack.

31. Decide on Location for Children to Sleep

While on a trip you might not always get a crib at your destination, and carrying one will make life all the more difficult. Instead call ahead to see if there are any cribs or roll out beds for children. You may even put blankets on the floor. Weave them a story about camping and they will gladly sleep without any trouble.

32. Get Baby Products Delivered At Your Destination

If you are absolutely paranoid about not getting your favourite variety of diaper or brand of baby food, check out online stores like amazon.com for services in your destination city. You can buy things online ahead of your travel and get them delivered to your hotel upon arrival.

33. Feeding Needs Of Your Infants

If you are travelling with a breastfed infant, you save the trouble of carrying bottles and bottle sanitization kits. For special food, or medications, you may need to call ahead to make sure you have a refrigerator where you are staying.

34. Feeding Needs of Your Toddler

With the progression from infancy to toddler, their dietary requirements too evolve. You will have to pack some snacks for travelling time. Fresh fruits and vegetables can be purchased at your destination. Most of the cities you travel to in whichever part of the world, will have baby food products and formulas, available at the local drug-store or the supermarket.

35. Picking Clothes for Your Baby

Contrary to popular belief, babies can do without many changes of clothes. At the most pack 2 outfits per day. Pack mix and match type clothes for your little one as well. Pick things which are comfortable to wear and quick to dry.

36. Selecting Shoes for Your Baby

Like outfits, kids can make do with two pairs of comfortable shoes. If you can get some water resistant shoes it will be best. To expedite drying wet shoes, you can stuff newspaper in them then wrap them with newspaper and leave them to dry overnight.

37. Keep One Change of Clothes Handy

Travelling with kids can be tricky. Keep a change of clothes for the kids and mum handy in your purse or tote bag. This takes a bit of space in your hand luggage but comes extremely handy in case there are any accidents or spills.

38. Leave Behind Baby Accessories

Baby accessories like their bed, bath tub, car seat, crib etc. should be left at home. Many hotels provide a crib on request, while car seats can be borrowed from friends or rented. Babies can be given a bath in the hotel sink or even in the adult bath tub with a little bit of water. If you bring a few bath toys, they can be used in the bath, pool, and out of water. They can also be sanitized easily in the sink.

39. Carry a Small Load Of Plastic Bags

With children around there are chances of a number of soiled clothes and diapers. These plastic bags help to sort the dirt from the clean inside your big bag. These are very light weight and come in handy to other carry stuff as well at times.

Pack with a Purpose

40. Packing for Business Trips

One neutral-colored suit should suffice. It can be paired with different shirts, ties and accessories for different occasions. One pair of black suit pants could be worn with a matching jacket for the office or with a snazzy top for dinner.

41. Packing for A Cruise

Most cruises have formal dinners, and that formal dress usually takes up a lot of space. However you might find a tuxedo to rent. For women, a short black dress with multiple accessory options will do the trick.

42. Packing for A Long Trip Over Different Climates

The secret packing mantra for travel over multiple climates is layering. Layering traps air around your body creating insulation against the cold. The same light t-shirt that is comfortable in a warmer climate can be the innermost layer in a colder climate.

Reduce Some More Weight

43. Leave Precious Things At Home

Things that you would hate to lose or get damaged leave them at home. Precious jewelry, expensive gadgets or dresses, could be anything. You will not require these on your trip. Leave them at home and spare the load on your mind.

44. Send Souvenirs by Mail

If you have spent all your money on purchasing souvenirs, carrying them back in the same bag that you brought along would be difficult. Either pack everything in another bag and check it in the airport or get everything shipped to your home. Use an international carrier for a secure transit, but this could be more expensive than the checking fees at the airport.

45. Avoid Carrying Books

Books equal to weight. There are many reading apps which you can download on your smart phone or tab. Plus there are gadgets like Kindle and Nook that are thinner and lighter alternatives to your regular book.

Check, Get, Set, Check Again

46. Strategize Before Packing

Create a travel list and prepare all that you think you need to carry along. Keep everything on your bed or floor before packing and then think through once again – do I really need that? Any item that meets this question can be avoided. Remove whatever you don't really need and pack the rest.

47. Test Your Luggage

Once you have fully packed for the trip take a test trip with your luggage. Take your bags and go to town for window shopping for an hour. If you enjoy your hour long trip it is good to go, if not, go home and reduce the load some more. Repeat this test till you hit the right weight.

48. Add a Roll Of Duct Tape

You might wonder why, when this book has been talking about reducing stuff, we're suddenly asking you to pack something totally unusual. This is because when you have limited supplies, duct tape is immensely helpful for small repairs – a broken bag, leaking zip-lock bag, broken sunglasses, you name it and duct tape can fix it, temporarily.

49. List of Essential Items

Even though the emphasis is on packing light, there are things which have to be carried for any trip. Here is our list of essentials:

- Passport/Visa or any other ID

- Any other paper work that might be required on a trip like permits, hotel reservation confirmations etc.
- Medicines – all your prescription medicines and emergency kit, especially if you are travelling with children
- Medical or vaccination records
- Money in foreign currency if travelling to a different country
- Tickets- Email or Message them to your phone

50. Make the Most of Your Trip

Wherever you are going, whatever you hope to do we encourage you to embrace it whole-heartedly. Take in the scenery, the culture and above all, enjoy your time away from home.

On a long journey even a straw weighs heavy.

-Spanish Proverb

>TOURIST

Facundo Iglesia

>TOURIST

Packing and Planning Tips

A Week before Leaving

- Arrange for someone to take care of pets and water plants
- •Stop mail and newspaper
- Notify Credit Card companies where you are going.
- Change your thermostat settings
- Car inspected, oil is changed, and tires have the correct pressure.
- Passports and id is up to date.
- Pay bills.
- Copy important items and download travel Apps.
- Start collecting small bills for tips

Right Before Leaving

- Clean out refrigerator.
- Empty garbage cans.
- Lock windows.
- Make sure you have the right ID with you.
- Bring cash for tips.
- Remember travel documents.
- Lock door behind you.
- Remember wallet.
- Unplug items in house and pack chargers.

Facundo Iglesia

Read other Greater Than a Tourist Books

Greater Than a Tourist San Miguel de Allende Guanajuato Mexico: 50 Travel Tips from a Local by Tom Peterson

Greater Than a Tourist – Lake George Area New York USA: 50 Travel Tips from a Local by Janine Hirschklau

Greater Than a Tourist – Monterey California United States: 50 Travel Tips from a Local by Katie Begley

Greater Than a Tourist – Chanai Crete Greece: 50 Travel Tips from a Local by Dimitra Papagrigoraki

Greater Than a Tourist – The Garden Route Western Cape Province South Africa: 50 Travel Tips from a Local by Li-Anne McGregor van Aardt

Greater Than a Tourist – Sevilla Andalusia Spain: 50 Travel Tips from a Local by Gabi Gazon

Greater Than a Tourist – Kota Bharu Kelantan Malaysia: 50 Travel Tips from a Local by Aditi Shukla

Children's Book: Charlie the Cavalier Travels the World by Lisa Rusczyk

Facundo Iglesia

> TOURIST

Visit Greater Than a Tourist for Free Travel Tips
http://GreaterThanATourist.com

Sign up for the Greater Than a Tourist Newsletter for discount days, new books, and travel information:
http://eepurl.com/cxspyf

Follow us on Facebook for tips, images, and ideas:
https://www.facebook.com/GreaterThanATourist

Follow us on Pinterest for travel tips and ideas:
http://pinterest.com/GreaterThanATourist

Follow us on Instagram for beautiful travel images:
http://Instagram.com/GreaterThanATourist

Facundo Iglesia

> TOURIST

Please leave your honest review of this book on Amazon and Goodreads. Please send your feedback to GreaterThanaTourist@gmail.com as we continue to improve the series. Thank you. We appreciate your positive and constructive feedback. Thank you.

Facundo Iglesia

NOTES

>TOURIST

Printed in Great Britain
by Amazon